ENTER THE HEART OF THE FIRE

A Collection of Mystical Poems

ENTER THE HEART OF THE FIRE

A Collection of Mystical Poems

Edited by
MARY E. GILES
KATHRYN HOHLWEIN

A Book Issue of *Studia Mystica*
California State University
Sacramento, California

CONTENTS

Foreword by Mary E. Giles and Kathryn Hohlwein /13

Introduction: The Poem as Anamnesis
David Adams Leeming /17

Ken McCullough
Enter The Heart of the Fire /25
Evening /26
The Tracker /28

Bob Boldman
My Lord's Necklace /29
The Wings of St. Francis /34

David Denny
The Black /35

Raymond Roseliep
Of Wings /36

David Ray
The Return /38

Leonard Robinson
Ode to Light /40
In That Mysterious Event /43
Hard Questions to Some Animals, With Answers /44
Hymn to Dread /46

Patricia Goedicke
The Wind of Our Going: Adagio Ma Non Troppo /47

Dennis Schmitz
Solitude /50
What If Is What Is /52

Sri Chinmoy
 It Steals Into My Heart /53
 The Message of Surrender /54
 In Secrecy Supreme /55
 Alas, Then Why? /56
 Far, very far /56
 Between Nothingness and Eternity /57

Jeremy Ingalls
 Shadow Shift /58
 Evensong /59
 Glass Parable /60

Steven Lautermilch
 Sorrow /61
 The Little Hours /62

Daniel E. Davis
 The Whiteness of the Air /64

Jacob Trapp
 Buddha in the Desert /66
 The Buddha's Silence /67
 Death of Buddha /68
 Nativity of Lao Tzu /69

Ravi Singh
 Night in New Mexico /70
 Subway /71

David Hopes
 Inquisition /72
 Lord, How Long Sunset /73
 The Earthly Beauty /74

About the Authors /77

About the Editors /79

ENTER THE HEART OF THE FIRE

Foreword

Thoughtful essay probes for the link between mystical experience and aesthetic creating, but the poem whispers, "There is no connective. All is one."

The poems in this collection remind us of the wisdom which graces all great lovers, whether they be poets or not. In the depths of living there are no connectives. There is only loving, a loving out of which and through which is born the identifiable act.

Do not ask the mystic to name the word or gesture that defines loving. For whether the language is poetry or painting, that which nurses the sick and consoles the dying, urges seedlings to growth or nourishes young minds, it is one. It is the language of loving.

Nor ought we ask the mystic to explain the process whereby the act came into being. Even using the word "process" violates the mystery of loving insofar as words have boundaries of meaning. Perhaps, though, we can speak about an "impulse" to act that "impels" the mystic to create poetry or serve fellow creatures.

The impulse is not planned; neither is that which is impelled. It is and the act is. Granted there are conscious acts of will and intellect that respond to the impulse and shape and refine it into particularity, but in such responses there is no calculation. Calculation has no place in loving. Awareness, openness and alertness do. Our loving is being aware, open and alert to the impulse, and our acts are specific responses to being aware, open and alert.

The poem and the hand of solace, in each we glimpse diversity and oneness in divine loving. In the poem we sense strength and delicacy, passion and calm, flow and repose. In the poem we encounter the limited and the limitless in the power of words. In the poem we are drawn into the center of its center where the paradox of its being is resolved in the paradox of Being.

The poem is not necessarily a better act of loving than, say, planting corn, but it is a unique one. So too is each poem in this collection unique, a special dark entry into the mystery of loving.

The essay is a prose indicator to the re-collecting that follows and it employs yet a different kind of language: Referring to specific poets and their art, the essay too is a response to the divine impulse. Through it and through the poems we may receive the gift to see in the dark clarity of mystical love that out of Oneness is created the one and through the one is revealed the One.

Mary E. Giles
Kathryn Hohlwein

INTRODUCTION
by
David Adams Leeming

The Poem as Anamnesis

"God . . . brought them unto Adam to see what he would call them: and whatsoever Adam called every living creature, that was the name thereof."

(Genesis)

"Everything is only a metaphor; there is only poetry."

(Norman O. Brown)

The poetic act is a recalling not only of individual experience but of the universal pattern-making process by which energy is freed from randomness to become form. It is a representation of the means by which we, as the "naming" organ of Earth's body, apprehend that process and make Creation conscious of itself.

> so much depends
> upon
>
> a red wheel
> barrow
>
> glazed with rain
> water
>
> beside the white
> chickens.

The prose sentence "so much depends upon a red wheelbarrow, glazed with rain water, beside the white chickens" conveys nothing when deprived of a particular context. So much what? we ask. Why a *red* wheelbarrow? Why *white* chickens? Yet William Carlos Williams' "The Red Wheelbarrow" is effective precisely because it lacks particular context. It is a systematic molding of tired patterns, of habitual ways of non-seeing in limiting context, into a new, living pattern of seeing in unrestricted context, context that exists everywhere and nowhere. We are forced to see the red wheel, the glazing rain, and the whiteness as poems in themselves, related to barrow, water, and chickens in the world of prose but alive on their own as poetry. Poetry here is literally dis-covered in prose, and, of course, "much depends upon" our ability to find significant life in the apparently mundane. That is, much depends upon it if we are to be namers, if we are to realize our human potential.

If prose is the language by which we normally communicate, poetry is intended to carry us beyond normal communication to a glimpse of Essence itself. Poetry tells us that everything around us is metaphor for that essence. The great lyric brings harmony to chaos and we suddenly see as if for the first time.

> I placed a jar in Tennessee,
> And round it was, upon a hill.
> It made the slovenly wilderness
> Surround that hill.
>
> The wilderness rose up to it,
> And sprawled around, no longer wild.
> The jar was round upon the ground
> And tall and of a port in air.
>
> It took dominion everywhere.
> The jar was gray and bare.
> It did not give of bird or bush,
> Like nothing else in Tennessee.
>
> (Wallace Stevens
> "Anecdote of the Jar")

As S.R. Hopper has said, the poem "'assembles' things into 'world.'" We are taken through the masks of earth to a revelation of the true and hidden reality. Great poetry, then, is always mystical, if mysticism is the discipline of union with "ultimate reality" — the art of breaking through the barriers of time and space to a transcendent stasis. Poetry, in the words of T.S. Eliot,

> may effect revolutions in sensibility such as are periodically needed; may help to break up the conventional modes of perception and valuation which are perpetually forming, and make people see the world afresh, or some new part of it. It may make us from time to time a little more aware of the deeper, unnamed feelings which form the substratum of our being, to which we rarely penetrate; for our lives are mostly a constant evasion of ourselves, and an evasion of the visible and sensible world.[1]

Poetry must have always been a primary vehicle for this recollection or *anamnesis*. It is not difficult to imagine the original poets as shaman-like beings whose utterings were the runes of the invisible. It was surely they who composed and spoke in the special ritual language — the words which because of that formal arrangement could be heard by the powers, words which were metaphors for cosmic Being.

> Being a poet
> I sing: my song
> grafts buds to those branches
> Forests of flowers
> rise, deep
> fragrant perfumes
>
> The flowers are dancing:
> the deep perfume
> moves to the beat of a drum
>
> Dew globules
> thicken with life
> and run down the stems
> (From Jerome Rothenberg, trans.,
> "The Flowering War" (Aztek))

And poetry remains today the ambiguous language of mystery and significance. We do not properly search first for the literal meaning of the poem any more than we concern ourselves ultimately with the literal meaning of ritual words, as to do so would be to break the tone, to destroy the rune, to imply that the poet might better have used prose. Rather, we accept the ambiguity – as of an oracle – and we allow ourselves to relate to the significance it recollects. We allow ourselves to be drawn into a meditative participation in the particular poem's "uniqueness" and in the poetic process itself. We study process in the context which is the poem. In this connection Jung spoke of poetry as "the primordial image" translated into the "language of the present" and of the poet as the person who, consciously or unconsciously aware of the primordial image, attempts to re-establish contact between that image and mankind.

It should be pointed out that while this is in some sense a religious process it has nothing to do with organized religion or with the conventional symbols of organized religion. The question here is not "devotional" poetry. Even the great devotional poets – poets such as Eliot, Donne, and Hopkins – need to be approached as part of a broader vision of the sacred if we are to comprehend the significance of their works on more than a sectarian level. There is no doubt that for the Christian, poems such as Donne's Holy Sonnets or even Eliot's "Four Quartets" are particularly moving as in some sense devotional poems, but for the Christian as well as the non-Christian they are great poems because their ultimately mystical significance transcends the meaning of their sectarian symbols and allusions.

Consider, for example, Eliot's "Journey of the Magi." From the devotional or sectarian perspective we read the Magi story of the Book of Matthew for the meaning it contains – the theological meaning of the Gentiles entering the Hebrew world to discover the Christ child. But Eliot is able to retell the Magi story with sufficient originality of syntax and diction to carry us beyond the boundaries of the old context to a re-collection of a deeper myth with which the merely theological tale can not be directly concerned. This is the myth of the journey toward what William James called the "more" in human experience, the journey from disorder to harmony, chaos to creation, that has in one sense as its goal the symbols and words to contain and represent Logos (the Word).

The first five lines of "The Journey of the Magi" establish the theme of the night journey, a symbolic, spiritual process that occurs in the "very dead of winter" when we find ourselves at the lowest point, when the "ways" are "deep." The night journey is characterized by isolation; those around the questor are possessed by the prosaic, confining concerns – of the world: the camels are "sore-footed" and "refractory," the camel men think only of "their liquor and women," the cities are "hostile, the towns unfriendly." And within are the doubts based on nostalgic thoughts of a false, escapist "poetry," the tired sensual life of summer palaces, sherbert, and silken girls. Most of all, there are the doubts within, the voices "crying folly."

The second stanza marks an abrupt change. The cold of winter gives way to a "temperate valley . . . smelling of vegetation." A water-mill is "beating against the darkness." The quest leads from darkness to the garden of fertility, from the merely literal language and concerns of the road to a place of mysterious and non-contextualized symbols. Of course the old white horse, the three trees, the pieces of silver, can be read in Christian terms, but their universal significance arises from their being fruitful, that is, potentially energy-bearing and anamnestic. It is important precisely that the magus on his way to Bethlehem could not have known the meaning of the symbols of Christ's later life. For him the water-mill is not Christ's winnowing fan but the namer's enlightenment beating against the ever-present tendency toward dark, entropic sameness reflected in the ordinary failure to see the Word in that unexpected place which was "(you may say) satisfactory." One remembers the simple barnyard of "The Red Wheelbarrow." Williams' poem and Eliot's, like all serious poetry, are themselves metaphors to express the poetic-shamanic quest for runes – the symbols, metaphors, images, in which to contain the Word.

Written in the year of Eliot's conversion to Anglo-Catholicism the Magi poem reflects in a particularly personal way a poetic and mystical process which, only after profound doubts, would culminate in the bringing together of words and the Word at the end of the "Four Quartets."

> And all shall be well and
> All manner of thing shall be well
> When the tongues of flame are in-folded
> Into the crowned knot of fire
> And the fire and the rose are one.

The final stanza of "The Journey of the Magi" is a meditation on the process which has already taken place, the stanza in which the hero

chooses to go beyond the central event of his adult life to a confronta-
tion with death which will lift his discovery or art out of time and
space to cosmos. The magus-poet is now literally dictating words:

> . . . but set down
> This set down
> This: . . .

And like anyone whose life has been overwhelmed and radically
altered by a vision of Logos fully articulated in the primary world, he
finds himself – again like the newly converted poet himself – lost in a
world dominated by "the old dispensation," a world of the desperate
and ignorant "clutching their gods," their tired conventions, empty of
creative energy.

Was the discovery of the event in the merely "satisfactory" place a
birth into new life as one would have hoped, having been "led all this
way?" Or was it somehow death? Later in "Four Quartets" Eliot
would discover it was both in the mystical paradox of "in my begin-
ning is my end" and "in my end is my beginning." To die to the old life
is to be born into the new. "I should be glad of another death" speaks
to the sense of fear and doubt that comes from loneliness brought
about by higher knowledge and to the realization that that
knowledge must be made operative in the unseeing prosaic world of
palaces, surly camel men, idol worshippers, and material temptations
to which the magi and all the "converted" must return. "Another
death" would imply total death to this world and total reception into
a truer one. The last line recalls that the poetic quest which in Eliot's
view is a religious process of sacrifice and death: "the progress of an
artist is a continual self-sacrifice, a continual extinction of personality"
culminating in union with Logos itself in that other death.[2]

The same quest is evident in more secular poems such as "The Red
Wheelbarrow" or "Anectode of the Jar" where the poets in question
discover suddenly that numinosity found by the magi in the strange
place of birth. Williams and Stevens, too, without the assistance of
Eliot's Christian symbols, arrive at the impersonality and self-sacrifice
of fully objective obeisance to the sacred center in all things. As
"priests of the invisible" they, too, re-collect the eternal poem.

---

1. T.S. Eliot, *The Use of Poetry and the Use of Criticism* (London, 1964), p. 155.
2. T.S. Eliot, *Selected Essays* (London, 1951), p. 17.

Enter the Heart of the Fire

When St. Alonzo staggered through the shallows
he did not see, at first, the questions
in concentric circles, nor the players in completion.
He fell more slowly as he continued not to speak;
a slave by any other gate would take precautions.
Just before his Self's extinction he found the grotto.
Overhead, through hewn passageways
he finally knew their language, then
getting into the boat, the leather of their bodies.
Each of his senses stationed around him
as statues he could barely gloss.
He was not entitled to bloat upon his own devotion;
no time to congratulate, no time to weep.
Free to be loved, he rose above the gardens.

Evening

And then,
my dear,
came acceptance.
Then came
hours, days, and
an end of resurrection.
You slept
in the country,
crystal warbler
withholding life.
Singular,
fallible,
you drank
the mating sycamores
the cloud drifts –
a drink
too heady
to be denied.
Rejoiced,
despite it,
despite the pastels
shredded
by the life-breath
of the farmhouse.
To come,
as we come,
to the full table.
Such a long wait.

Such a
winning over
of terrors
from the mutable.
And then
such a deep
opening
of the moonlight.

The Tracker

Saying this, he undid his braided belt
and set the whole field ablaze.
Alonzo the Listener saw this from a distance.
His lip twitched. He turned and knelt to drink
from the turquoise of the glacier run-off.

He'd tracked him for seven years
Eating only grubs and injured goshawks.
Mornings, the fox barked his doxology
Nights in the timber: weather.

Yesterday he watched a dappled spaniel
move in circles of uncertainty
stop, woodcut in the snowlight –
Not the full moon, but The Other One, perched
in the smoky vertebrae of the ridge
annointing the sky with blood.

My
Lord's
Necklace

16
tanka

i have no voice
but His
He breaks my body
and violets blossom

silence
wraps and fills
the hand
my Lord stretches tight
the sky

resting here
there is nowhere to go
nothing to do
accepting Him
i leave the window open
for the rain

rain
on the temple
steps
a prayer
from the yellow river

my Lord
reaches His Hand
and the sea
brings
wave after wave

                              i will give you a hint
                              call Him
                              and He is silent
                              move
                              and He is space

                              stars, stars
                              and the shadow of night
                              fits into me
                              as i wait
                              i hold His Silence

sitting
i follow my breath
out to where
the wind
meets the hazel pine

someday
i will die
and disappear
into these
poems

moving with the breath
there is only
a hair's difference
between emptiness
and the ordinary mind

molding the stars
smoothing the emptiness
the Hand
of my Lord

because i am
this body
i accept Christ

because i am
formless
i accept Buddha

one, one
everything
within
and without

countless
stars
they are beads
in my Lord's
necklace

love Him
and do not sleep
His long shadow
leans into
my dream

with a rope
i lower the sun
water the garden
and speak to
my Lord

The Wings of St. Francis

the fireflies fly
     behind the stained glass
     saints

on a bible
  the moth opens   &closes
    paper-thin wings

counting the beads
       the bees
hum

out of the blue
    a bluejay
    on the statue of st. francis

    (for father raymond roseliep, 1981)

The Black

My Stallion! Heart, my far-off, pounding core,
My Courage, where, beneath which rim of rock,
Within what wash, across what canyon floor
Do you pace and rear, a captive, locked

In love for me, and waiting? How, oh how
Could I have lost you? Now my veins are dry
Arroyos, flaming for your blood, and now,
My Heart, my Spring, without your slaking eyes

My breast is burning desert, vast as sky.
My bones are strange to me. My body thrives
In you and dies through nights without you. Cry!
And pound the earth, your voice and pulse, two knives

To wound me into action, not to kill
Me. Guide me into your abyss, through plains
Of pain, down switchback, broken paths until
I reach the stream. And there, beneath the stains

Of blood and lather, I will see your might,
Your muscles glisten in the copper canyon.
I will drink you, taste my life, find light
Within your jet-black mane, my dark companion.

And I will be a home, a tent where you
May live, and you will come forever, call
Me to my feet and lead me, gallop to
The shore and give me all your sea, your All.

Of Wings

bird landing
sky color
on its face

name
to the wind
breath on wing

hummingbird zing
taking a child
to hear

larks take
the air
you took

                                    wild geese in my eyes
                                       earth swings
                                          off its axis

magnolia nightingale
          I slip out
          of my skin

                                          owl:
                                          our
                                          whoness

The Return

The old lady saw that in
her lifetime the mountains
had been moved about
and one was missing
altogether. She knew it
for she was taken back
and she saw that one peak
was where another had been
and that on the water
beyond blue waves were further
apart and sky was joined
with earth at a different
level   with the seam more
broken and jagged yet
she also knew there was no
point in babbling of this
that no one would listen.
The only valid thoughts
were in the secret caverns
of her self and there was not
much of that self left.
She touched her parched lip.
She saw that the pool
that formerly was directly
between two mountains
was distanced now at least
a mile but she did not
smile and ask to be helped
to bend to this pool and taste

to see if any sign within
perhaps the taste of ash
would let her know
secretly what had happened
some unnoticed and unreported
volcanic action. They could
chalk up her desire to drink
to be lowered to the blue
water   to an old lady's
eccentricity. She tasted
what her hand bore
to her lips but found nothing
changed – it was still
the clear and intriguing
tastelessness of her untried
girlhood. She looked up.
Has anything unusual happened
around here lately? Have you heard
of anything? There was no
answer and she knew silence
to be negation. The fleecy
clouds floated over calmly.
Nothing had happened at all.
Her life had come and gone but
that was not much to
talk about. She was ready
as a deer at that water.
She remembered her mother's face.

Ode To Light

– 1 –

I lie here
at the bottom
of night
like a trout
and I know
your secret, Light.

– 2 –

First, master of image, I will tell of your
soon-coming dawn, reflect how still once more
your elephants of broken silk will come massing
in our corners, the color of laughing as your crowny pikes,

rose-gold, ascend the stage and the wild dance of day begins
from the horizon. Smooth fleer on all roads now you will flood
our diamond globe with massive flowering and paint again the
egret's royal maneuvers and his hopes. Tripping among

pools of shadow, model of all laughter, Clown, bouncing, toppling
off the roof of heaven, off the wall and through my window,
bluebird, through my window in your invisible
world-suit, splitting in two at tree trunks, expression –

less, clown-cheek fiery, shattering among a million leaves,
mocking the timid wind his roaring wholeness, his silly groans,
with tripping mottles, turning wind-sighs to laughter, to seen
arpeggios from your vast bag of counterpoint, your infinite

music-box of shade. Armies of starlings will kiss you open –
mouthed, and the nightingale who has learned to tell your beauty
back in sound, and does, from her tree, to hold you, try to hold you,
wild visitor, when, at each day's end you turn twirling

your peacock cape of twilight, aster-lined, to leave us. Moctezuma
trembled like the nightingale and kept his singers up all night for
he could well imagine a king-caused dark forever. What can be
imaged can be so. You, juggler of reflection, taught him that.

– 3 –

But your secret; you travel unenchanted
through the darkness; I see you, clear as day,
holding your breath as you shuttle, bored
as time through space, look straight ahead
not right or left. Until you reach us. Then,
click, we turn you on and then you flood us
with your self, hold nothing back. I see you,
arriving, breathe again. Home. House that sunlight
built. You love the earth. You love us. Secret   clear
                    as day.

– 4 –

Our heads are small suns, moon-
round; thought is ray-like, all-flooding
reflective, refractive, quick as shadow,
mimetic as shadow, vault of laughter. Our
eyes see seven hues, all you bring, the
sum of the transparent, and you
are emperor here, creator of all
that is seen, seen through; creator of
we who see you and our palaces.

41

Purloined Answer
are you an envoy?
Can we take your
single-minded
travelling
as a sign?

Beloved Light
none here
laugh at
Moctezuma
now. En-
force your
laughter,
teach us to live in
opalescent
castle, all
window open
all wall a
see-through
walk-through
glistening always
upstairs
downstairs
through the dark night's
dangers.

In That Mysterious Event

In that mysterious event
first hands break into feeling
and then along the skin
the million-year-old eyes,
numberless, open
like pond lillies;

next the heart breaks into blossom
as if into fire;

then last, the day-closed flower of grief
breaks into metaphorless flame
and is consumed,
leaving no slightest trace,
as if it had not been
nor even been imagined.

Hard Questions To Some Animals, With Answers

Why do you nibble and pray and
nibble all over the clover, rabbit?

> "Clover is the sun."

Why do you eat the high-jumping eland and
why do you eat the almost-flying eland, great cat?

> "Eland is the sun."

Why, dog, do you look at me as though I were
God? Why do your eyes follow me with a
saint's adoration of God? *You* know that *I*
know you're hardly spiritual, that you
concentrate on food almost to the total
exclusion of everything else.

> "Food is the sun."

The sun! The sun! Can't you answer with anything
else? Do you think the sun is God? That God is a total
materialist? Does he mean nothing more to you than

food? Well, answer me. All of you. Is the food-giving
sun God?

> "No. The sun is a messenger."

A messenger? A messenger? And what is its so holy
message then? Eat? Go thou and eat?

> "Oh, no. Be full."

Be full? That's the messenger's message from
God? That's *it*? That's the whole thing? Be full?

"No. Also, be not empty."

hymn to dread

i know, Lord, i have awe of You hidden in me
like a mortal sin   Musk Of The Frozen
Himalayas In Rose, i know i tremble in my belly
at You. though they hold their smiling Logic

up and swing its huge grin before us all like
an incense pot to still our awful terror of Thee
and loose our hidden grasp upon Thee, Royal
Palm of Time, i am glued against the duty of Your Body.

they need to kill us, Lord, for eternity. last
night that dr. hummingbird with his gigantic sweet-
ness needle lulled me and softened me and when i
tried to sing to You, oh Violet In Music Like

Water, oh Pterodactyl Of The Hidden Moon, my notes
froze in my throat, my clutching fingers slid off the side
of heaven's flank and i heard Your Voice inside
me far off as in a tomb. they bury You. o blast

them with an unheard note, Musk Of Small Snow Roar-
ing In The Andes, Terrible Hand In The Window Of
Knowing, blow out past every inwardness of Pterodactyl
Of The Hidden Sun, and let, oh Lord, Thy Kingdom Come.

The Wind of Our Going: Adagio Ma Non Troppo

Everything in motion!
                              No

Yes, it is
So, even in the blood

Cells veer and
Shift like minnows

Silver, swimming up
Stream and then down,

When I went out

For a short walk and came
Back home everything

Was gone!
                    Soft sand

On a beach blows

From one day
To the next,
                    the grasses

Ripple and disappear

But come back
Again

We will smile,
Speak,
      again

The energy

Of each atom,
If we should ever

Die, no!
        The heated

Wind of our going passes

Above us,
        into the trees

The irregular shadows
Fall

On a white wall,
          ribbons

Of blown sand, fluid

Branches weave and
Flow, the wooden arms

Even of a chair have it,

The molecules heave but
Still change,

As on a bright October
Gusty day the yellow

Little oval leaves shower

Pieces of pure
Yellow glitter, even

When both of us
                    are gone

In the slow movement

Of a Bach Prelude, the ocean
On a gray day

Becalmed

Still the music pours,
The light

Yellow hooves
Of the harpsichord

Keep rippling and weaving

Over the cellos,
The dark

Machine of the universe, the deep

Buzz of wood
                    in motion.

Solitude

I would not make the hole larger.
for hours I looked
through the dot I started

with a thumbnail on the black loft window:
Wabash down to the river,
Chicago sky & rooftops angle into dark.

all day pigeons softly thrash the glass
on the other side.
I imitate them with sooty hands –

for a long weekend I will not wash
this blackness
but scratch more at the glass,

wanting camouflage
or familiar pigment, negative –
a way to give weight to my hands.

at night I can come down,
a man with no gift for solitude
forced to ask for it,

& walk, because of the dark, unreflected
by the storefront windows.
& smile at the mannikin anxiety

of the figures as they gesture
upstage at another's meaningless fashion,
smile at a toy-room, crib & the unused clothing

a mother would discard
as she prepares the would-be child
for sleep — none of it wrinkled, sweat-through

to a darker pigment.
& dream I am going blank,
my hair whitening, showing the visibility

the body sheds.
at night I imagine glass around my hands,
that I am breathing clouds

onto the glass around my head.
my color drains as I fingerprint the walls,
the storefronts with soot.

What If Is What Is

the mind you can think of crab-walks
over the wet surface,
can sort out the bad lentil

when reason is reason enough
not to eat.
but the counter-mind fills —

a pebble is enough, star joined to star —
or New York glassed in,
maybe blasphemous force, the line of sewer
covers slick in midnight

rain twenty blocks across 63rd,
an obsession —
other islands man has rescued, destinies
more simple, dialects more involved,
but each an instant

an increase failing exhaustion.
the Bronx Park monkeys scream
out of the nether world;
a human distance seems atrocious.

with prehensile fingers we pick up motes
strained out by fur arguing
the context for epiphany rather than epiphany.

It Steals into My Heart

There was a time when I loved
The fantastic fabrics of the mind.
There was a time
When I lived my life
Based on culled fictions.
There was a time
When I was satisfied
With a fragment of reality,
Splintered, broken and smashed.
But now a lucid illumination
Steals into my heart.
The eternal Presence
Of Infinity's Light
Feeds my Vision's Dawn.

The Message of Surrender

Today You have given me
The message of surrender.
I have offered to You
My very flower-heart.
In the dark night with tears,
In the unknown prison-cell of illusion,
In the house of the finite,
No longer shall I abide.
I know You are mine.
I have known this Mother,
O Queen of the Eternal.

In Secrecy Supreme

In secrecy supreme I see You.
You live in my eyes, in my sleep,
In my dreams, in my sweet wakefulness.
In the stupendous mirth of life,
In the abysmal lap of death,
You I behold.
Your Love-Play is my world.

Alas, Then Why?

By whose touch does the lily smile
And open its beauty-bud?
Whose moonlit beauty
Do I see in the lily?
Who is the Eye of my eye;
Who is the Heart of my heart?
Alas, then why do I not see Him,
His face of transcendental Beauty,
Even in my dreams?

Far, very far,
Near, very near
I hear Your ankle bells.
Why do I lose my self-form in shyness?
How long have I to wait for You
To tie my hands
With Your love-cord?

Between Nothingness and Eternity

Barren of events,
Rich in pretensions
My earthly life.

Obscurity
My real name.

Wholly unto myself
I exist.

I wrap no soul
In my embrace.

No mentor worthy
Of my calibre
Have I.

I am all alone
Between failure and frustration.

I am the red thread
Between Nothingness
And Eternity.

Shadow Shift

In sunlight, moonlight, all of us
Walk with long shadows.
A wind-blown tree casts shadows also.
A stronger light sustains; its trellis binds
Suns, moons, and trees, and us, and here this vine
Named for the Passion of Christ.
Pasque flowers cast long shadows too on wind-spun earth in earth-lights.

Twenty-four moons had passed before our young one noticed,
Became alarmed at swaying, moon-cast shadows.
Under the tree in the wind he clung to our knees for comfort.
That night he has forgotten now but from that night he knows
Shadows portend no harm for those
Borne on a swifter wind that blows
Past stars and moons from light far past all starlights.

Evensong

Coyotes gnaw and scorpions strike
Groping arm and stumbled foot.
Starfire lends scant ballast to these wars.
Earth's moon, chief satellite to coyote's barking,
Grants no more than man-wired metals shape
Of light succinct enough for scorpion-scouting.
Cupped candles gut in glutted wax.
Neighbor windows darken,
And certain as uncertain dark the heart
Alerts to coyote moonwatch, scorpion stealth,
To decadence of stars, galactic sieges.
But here in this same house a sound more vast
Than roar of five world galaxies invades
And light no candle-rate nor light-beam measures.
Outsounding desert yelp, assaulting years
With firm impalpable erasures, bell
And candle borne of cause without a gauge
Sound and search all thresholds. Of this dark
The heart, ascending curfew, dares relearn
                Sempiternal evensong.

Glass Parable

Earth's salt seas and sky's galactic seas
Are all one sea and one reflecting glass
    On which, in which, we pass
        Within, among
The changing fires, fires purging, fires destroying.

      Variously these fires
    Fuse, defuse, refuse all seas
  On which, through which, we pass
       Into the strong
Sea of fire which there beyond the glass
Shrives the quantum born beyond destroying.

Sorrow

and with what strength receive his ghost.
The ankles unfolding. The knees.
Below the thighs blossoming unwinding the right arm
sending out that hand. Bud of stone.

Loins. Elbows. Fingertips. Cheekbones. Mouth.
Slow leaves along a pure dark bloom.
Flowering no more than breathing in breathing out.
Having to open, close to shadow.

Melting beneath the keel of the ribs.
So much like flood waters rising, washing to go down.
And leave land dry and from the sea form creatures that live
and do not drown.

The light within these eyes this face
made so deep in peace, so full of grace.

The Little Hours

Matins

Oh, your whitening skin
wrinkling in cold morning light
and that good eye winking

Prime

Along the aisles of the city, from car door and window
sun spiders, star widows
light the old tapers, watch the new candles dance

Terce

Below the paved streets, under horns and pipes
the pilots of the subways, their passengers
steer through the darkness, move upon the deep

Sext

Sharp, the pull and the plunge
clattering on bright stones:
the exhaling sweet, close

Nones

Over the tiles of crop and field, the grouting of highway and track
the shadow of wings
passes without leaving a trace

Vespers

Down the rows of corn, around the whorls of baled hay
first the cricket then the firefly
come from the pockets of the evening, join the hands of the night

Compline

The double rhythm of your heart
closing, closing
the darkness of that game eye letting you sleep

The Whiteness of the Air

The whiteness of the air is
as the whiteness of the whale,
drifting in the dark
like the aimless, airy
flotsom of some vain explorer.
The cold is couched in loneliness,
and the crunch of my bootsoles vanishes
into the gentleness of the downfall sky.
The stark trees stand
like Chinese characters
inked on clean rice paper
concealing an alien message
from the East,
but fade beneath the weight of the shifting
white air that settles slowly
over automobiles and neon signs.

It calls to me,
this cold white quiet
that sucks all to blankness,
and envelopes sounds and thickens actions
in its eager emptiness.
The wind is cold,
and it lifts the white about me
like a shroud.
I am lost in a momentary swirl,
and there is freedom here,
because all is gone
all is bleached away,

and I am left empty – for a moment –
and return pale, appalled
at the world
and my appetite.

Buddha in the Desert

As Sakya Muni sits motionless
on a shoreless sea of sand
the gods look down and envy him
his wisdom,
his consenting to stone.
The swallows that nested
in his outstretched hands
flew off one day,
following the call to distant lands.
Then the Tathagata,
who in his desert detachment
had seemingly stilled every desire,
began to weep.
So it is that flowers spring from rock.

The Buddha's Silence

Saffron-robed monks
in convocation at Benares,
greedy for jewels of Buddha-wisdom,
eagerly awaited Siddhartha's coming.
The Tathagata came.
Before a hushed congregation,
all ears,
he stood silently holding up
a flower for them to contemplate.
Om mani padme hum.

Death of Buddha

Ananda tending
the dying Buddha's
couch under the twin
Sala trees,
saw the awed wood's wintry
buds break into bloom,

and, bending low,
spread over him
whose cool compassionate hand
allayed the world's
fevered pulse,
petals of fragrant snow.

Nativity of Lao Tzu

Blue over the May-month plum tree
deepened to violet in the abrupt
anguish of birth pains,

the nine years times nine of being
great with child dwindled and merged,
as Lao's mother, to whom

the swift gentle unicorn came
in a swirl of plum blossoms,
gave birth to a man-child, haloed

with soft hair white as bleached
silk in sunlight, a seer ancient
among ancient seers,

his face a wrinkled parchment Tao
had written wise, patient *yin*
deep in his *yang* eyes.

Night in New Mexico
for Donna

Espanola shimmers
In your eyes of far coyotes.
Your eyes almost turquoise.
Your blood roars in the riverbeds.
Your rainbow body not in gravity
Keeps us warm from harm.
Your longing is a shooting star
Aiming for the All.
Your hair is the beautiful wind.
Your mind is a mystery school.
In your breathing a desert flowers.
Your heart levitates the dark.
Your name is an enlightenment of snow.
Your soul hears the silence speak
And makes all secrets known.

Subway

I could say anything
And make it shine in the context of you.
If this trainride is my life
Make my rails mirrorlike.

I am reeling in the tunnel
Of worlds beyond worlds.
(We forget the dark with every stop.)

The conductor announces your names.
(He tells us when to change and grow.)

Motorman of my soul —
Don't take me back on myself.

End of the line be mine.

Inquisition

We will be asked. The Inquisitor
is curious in any weather,
hot on the scent of what we did
and whom we did it for.
Admit only this: we are lovely and we live forever.

That He who made us should not know
is final proof of whether
we were made in wisdom or delight.
He did not watch His sowing grow
away from Him, lovely, and to live forever.

> Some of us hid.
> Some of us passed
> into the voices of a beast or bird.
> Those of us who answered right
> added something to the Word.

I would have thought our sorrows earned
an hour of freedom from the measure.
No matter. What counts at last
is that someone lasting learned
we are lovely, and we live forever.

Lord, How Long Sunset

Lord, how long sunset and moonset
against the bare hill at my window?
How long springset, winterset against this heart
before it finds the opening, and flies?
If I were a fisher I would cast my net.
If I were a prophet I would know.
If I were a pilgrim I would start
wayfaring now before the longing dies.
I have thought and I have thought
and I gnarl to rest at last
where flesh and soul were poorly bought
with all the world high-stepping past.
Lord, You bring my certain soul to doubt,
spoil heart's home, that they must set out.

The Earthly Beauty

Plato knew it. Pythagoras knew it.
Augustine knew it, smitten by forms
    the Ghost breathed on:
    a golden head, a back bent just so to
blow all argument away,
Divine Mind walking in the Paradise of things,
    to touch, to taste and see.

Take off your clothes and I will decide what to believe.
Stand naked in the naked world.
    What's kingfisher wear, kindled between sky and water?
    What's stylish in the heaven of heavens
where the saints with their hosannas
flame like stars?
    Bare. God alone is bare of everything. But try.

If you are hurt or beautiful, I will
listen to your words
    for the sake of them who are
    hurt and beautiful:
Ellen of sorrows, whose boy voice sweetly
singing brings, as in some sweet old painting,
    angels, should there be angels;

Elaine, lynx-eye, Athena-eye, ice blue,
whose lashes are the doors of every delectation;
    Jane, whose downward midnight hair is
    fidelity and dalliance, arabesque and plane,
austerity and expenditure onto her cunning shoulders;
Katherine, at the contours of whose face
    the purposeful town gives up and sits down to sing;

Sara, whose chest is a heavenly fiction
where two suns are forever rising;
    Anne, whose collar-bone is the salvation of the world;
    Sally, whose moving is a gold nail in the heart;
Phoebe, whose bird feet go on by as though
we had not burst our souls inside us
    as she sailed the evening homage light.

Beauty of the flesh in them
is forever squandered and reborn,
    wrinkled, faceted, diverted and undone.
    Of all things it most moves, fills, yearns
for a further place, a changing and eternal home.
It is a smashing power, a curled fist. It shatters.
    It upholds. It has power to spend itself.

If you are beautiful and hurt I will
stay up late to make a poem in your honor.
    In it I will swear that soul wears body
    as a man his clothes according to the weather.
For the lifting of your hand at such an angle
I will give you temperance, integrity, magnanimity,
    fortitude, simplicity, and fire.

Let someone say .that beauty is the snare of hell
and I will cry the Virgin out of Angelico
    and Raphael and out of Paradise,
    and let them speak again
before that flesh afire,
that blood and bone
    the Ghost put on for glory.

I will pray, "Beauty, mother of virtue, be about us."
The heart does not leap
    unless it leaps to God.
    Who scorns Creation scorns Creator.
Who does not fall down and praise the gay-wings
in its bog is soul-dead. Who would not give all
    for spiderwort gets nothing.

As sun strikes tree, tree
sinks to coal, coal to rock,
    rock to diamond,
    and the diamond
leaps to fire again, so beauty in any shade
is that beauty that shall light Jerusalem.
    Therefore

for the runner bent forward in the crisis of the race,
for the young face thinking for a moment of
    something but itself,
    the radiant unconscious,
for them who steer lordly on the world
like ships in white rig of comeliness,
    for eye, flank, hair, curve, hollow,

hand, throat, foot, soul,
mystical, silly, perfect, the True Cross
    on which we suffer and are saved
    there is no propriety but praise.
We will trade tale for tale. We'll talk of anyone
who walked in loveliness beside us for a while,
who for the wisdom of their dust be sung forever.

76

About the Authors

Bob Boldman lives in Kettering, Ohio where he writes devotional poems and publishes in many magazines.

Sri Chinmoy, poet, author, musician and artist lives in New York where he lectures and offers concerts, poetry readings and meditations. Born in 1931 in East Bengal, India, he entered a spiritual community as a young child, spending 20 years in intensive prayer and meditation.

Daniel E. Davis presently teaches English and directs the Reading Program at St. John's Military Academy in Delafield, Wisconsin. He has published in several poetry magazines, including *Studia Mystica*, II, 1.

David Denny lives contemplatively at The Spiritual Life Institute community in Nova Scotia. He regularly publishes in *Desert Call*, a magazine put out by their community.

Patricia Goedicke is the author of five books of poetry, the most recent of which are *The Dog That Was Barking Yesterday* and *Crossing the Same River*. This fall she will teach at the University of Montana in Missoula. She and her husband, Leonard Robinson, spend most of their time in their home in San Miguel de Allende, Mexico.

David Hopes teaches at Syracuse University, runs, sings, is poet-in-residence at Westcott Cordial Shop, and is an amateur naturalist. He has published abundantly; more of his "Lord poems" are in *Studia Mystica*, III, 1.

Jeremy Ingalls, who lives in Tucson, Arizona, is the author of *The Metaphysical Sword, Tahl, The Galilean Way* and several other books, including translations from Chinese and Japanese. She has received numerous fellowships and awards. Other poems by her appear in *Studia Mystica*, II, 2 and III, 3.

Steven Lautermilch teaches English at the University of North Carolina, Greensboro, where he is completing a study of the role of Orpheus in Rilke's poetry. His translations of Rilke's poetry and his own poems are in a variety of journals, including *Studia Mystica*, I, 4.

David Adams Leeming, associate professor of English and Comparative Literature at the University of Connecticut in Storrs, is contributing editor for *Parabola* and the author of: *Mythology: The Voyage of the Hero; Flights: Readings in Magic, Mysticism, Fantasy and Myth;* and *Mythology.*

Ken McCullough, resident of Iowa City, Iowa, is a visual artist as well as a poet. His poems have appeared in several publications.

David Ray, whose *Tramp's Cup* poems won the William Carlos Williams Prize, has received an Indo-American Fellowship to spend the academic year at Rajasthan University in Jaipur, India. His *Selected Poems* is forthcoming from Scarecrow Press.

Leonard Robinson is a poet, short story writer and novelist whose latest book is *The Man Who Loved Beauty*. His most recent poems are in *New Letters* and *The New Yorker*.

Raymond Roseliep, whose newest book of poems is *Listen to Light,* publishes extensively. His "haiku of mu," some of which are in *Studia Mystica*, II, 3, recently came out in *The Still Point: Haiku of Mu.*

Dennis Schmitz, recipient of the Guggenheim award and other prizes, has published several volumes of poetry, including more recently *String* and *Goodwill, Inc.* He teaches creative writing at California State University, Sacramento.

Ravi Singh lives in New York City where he teaches yoga and meditation in many contexts. He is founder and editor of two small press poetry magazines, *Out There* and *Grand Union.*

Jacob Trapp, Unitarian minister and artist of living, is a much published poet. Poems by him appear in *Studia Mystica*, I, 4 and IV, 1. He is editor of *Modern Religious Poems.*

About the Editors

Mary E. Giles and Kathryn Hohlwein are professors of Humanities and Religious Studies at California State University, Sacramento where they edit the quarterly journal, *Studia Mystica*. They are currently collaborating on a book of essays to be published in the spring of 1982. Kathryn Hohlwein, poet and author, gives many poetry readings, and her book, *Touchstones,* will be published by Harper & Row in 1982. Mary E. Giles writes in the area of literature and spirituality and gives seminars on prayer. Her translation of Osuna's *Third Spiritual Alphabet* appears in the fall of 1981 with Paulist Press.

Enter the Heart of the Fire has been set in 11/14 Kennerley Old Style by Barlow Printing, Inc. Frederic Goudy, the prolific American type designer, completed this face in 1911 for a limited edition book published by Mitchell Kennerley. Although named after Kennerley, the design is loosely based on the traditional faces Jenson and Caslon. Taken individually some of its characters may seem awkward, but when seen together in copy they are transformed into a typeface of grace and warmth.